Remember
~Journal~

All Scripture taken from the King James Version which is in the Public Domain.

REMEMBER - JOURNAL

ISBN 978-0-9893101-3-0

Scripture taken from the New King James Version®. Copyright ©1982 by Thomas Nelson, Inc. Used by permission. All rights reserved.

©2013 by Adam LiVecchi. All rights reserved. This book is protected by the copyright laws of the United States of America. No part of this publication may be reproduced, stored in a retrieval system, or transmitted in any form or by any means electronic, mechanical, photocopying, recording, or otherwise, without the prior written permission of the publisher or under consentual agreement.

Printed in the United States of America.

First Printing: July 2013

For more information on how to order this book or any of the other materials We See Jesus Ministries offers please contact:

> We See Jesus Ministries
> www.WeSeeJesusMinistries.com

"Blessed are the poor in spirit: for theirs is the kingdom of heaven (Matthew 5:3)." When we are poor in spirit we possess what money cannot buy. Those who are poor in spirit recognize their need for Jesus and people. As we recognize our need for Jesus he immediately begins to meet that need with himself. Christ begins to align our values system with his. His priorities become our priorities. We begin to desire his will to be done on earth as it is in heaven. Above all things we begin to treasure Jesus. When we treasure Jesus, we value what he says and does enough to write it down. The more you value what Jesus says the more he will speak to you. The more you value what he does the more he will work through you. This journal was created to record the testimonies of the Lord in your life. When you are praying a specific prayer write it down, when it is answered write it down. If you make a mistake write it down and it will become a lesson learned. When God does something write it down. If you have goals write them down, achieve them in Jesus name and write it down. If you fall write down what tripped you up, get up and learn from your mistakes. Your relationship with God will grow as you write things down. Your relationships with people will grow if you learn from your mistakes. Remember that a key to staying tenderhearted is to remember what the Lord has done both in and through you. Those who remember stay tender, so write it down and remember all that Jesus does in your life through his Holy Spirit. So pay attention, write it down and enjoy Jesus today because tomorrow is not promised.

Your friend,
Adam LiVecchi

Then those who feared the Lord spoke to one another,
And the Lord listened and heard them;
So a book of remembrance was written before Him
For those who fear the Lord
And who meditate on His name.
Malachi 3:16

> "Those who are searching for God's will, will not find it if they are not surrendering their will."
>
> Adam LiVecchi
> (The Execution of Jesus Christ)

> "The word deals with where we are and where we are going."
>
> Adam LiVecchi
> (Listen.Learn.Obey)

> "Christ is formed in us as God speaks to us."
>
> Adam LiVecchi
> (Sitting at His Feet)

> "The revelation of Jesus Christ is what true believers live for and from."
>
> Adam LiVecchi
> (His Name is the Word of God)

> "If we do not remember what God has said, it becomes easy for the enemy to steal from us."
>
> Adam LiVecchi
> (Sitting at His Feet)

> "When someone is full of hope they are more interested in the future than in the past."
>
> Adam LiVecchi
> (Follow.Lead.Mentor)

"Iron sharpens iron, but never without friction."

Adam LiVecchi
(The Increase of His Government)

> "We receive revelation so that we change how we see, which helps us change how we live and view life."
>
> Adam LiVecchi
> (His Name is the Word of God)

"Don't follow signs and wonders, be one."

Adam LiVecchi
(Listen.Learn.Obey)

> "The cross is meant to kill the stuff in us that will later kill us if not dealt with."
>
> Adam LiVecchi
> (The Execution of Jesus Christ)

"There is no greater joy than to know God."

Adam LiVecchi
(Sitting at His Feet)

> "Authority is to cast out demons power is to heal sickness. Jesus paid for people to be free and healed."
>
> Adam LiVecchi

When Jesus walked the earth as a man, He demonstrated "God with us." When He hung on a cross, He demonstrated "God for us."

Aaron LiVecchi

> "The chief cornerstone of our house is Christ. The mortar that holds the house together is the obedience of our faith."
>
> Adam LiVecchi
> (Rediscovering the Prophetic)

"Everything in the Kingdom of God is under Jesus' complete leadership."

Adam LiVecchi
(The Increase of His Government)

> "The crucified life is about living with a predisposition to forgive people whether or not they ever say they are sorry."
>
> Adam LiVecchi
> (Follow.Lead.Mentor)

> "When the word of God breaks in on a heart or mind, what was dark and obscure becomes illuminated and clear."
>
> Adam LiVecchi
> (Listen.Learn.Obey)

"God really believes in us and trusts us, therefore, we should start believing and trusting one another."

Adam LiVecchi
(Sitting at His Feet)

"There is no competition in the Kingdom"

Adam LiVecchi
(Go.Preach.Heal)

"Jesus said to deny yourself. God wouldn't tell you to do something that He wouldn't do."

Adam LiVecchi
(The Execution of Jesus Christ)

> "Jesus paid for us to have the mind of Christ by His crown of thorns."
>
> Adam LiVecchi
> (His Name is the Word of God)

> "As we rightly divide the word of truth, it rightly divides us."
>
> Adam LiVecchi
> (Listen.Learn.Obey)

> "When our motives are pure, transparency comes naturally."
>
> Adam LiVecchi
> (Follow.Lead.Mentor)

> "When we surrender our will, we are positioning ourselves for God's will which is defined clearly in His word."
>
> Adam LiVecchi
> (His Name is the Word of God)

> "Truth can never be compromised in the name of love."
>
> Adam LiVecchi
> (Go.Preach.Heal)

"The Father invested in you so you would learn to invest in yourself."

Aaron LiVecchi

> "Let's briefly define true prophetic ministry. God says something, we do it and they see him."
>
> Adam LiVecchi
> (Rediscovering the Prophetic)

> "The Secret Place is a life hidden in Christ."
>
> Adam LiVecchi
> (So You Want To Change The World)

> "If people do not see your integrity they will not want to hear your truth."
>
> Adam LiVecchi

> "Many people want a Savior, but very few want a Lord."
>
> Adam LiVecchi
> (Go.Preach.Heal)

> "Prophecy or prayer without action is merely verbalized unbelief."
>
> Adam LiVecchi
> (Rediscovering the Prophetic)

"Prudence is very important. Foresight can save you from needing to use insight."

Aaron LiVecchi

> "God wants our ears and our eyes to see what He has for us, because Jesus did, and He is our example in all things."
>
> Adam LiVecchi
> (Sitting at His Feet)

> "Sanctification is our conscience learning how to properly relate to the new creation."
>
> Adam LiVecchi

"If we want access to our inheritance, we must move forward with Jesus. We have to stop looking to the past to define our future."

Adam LiVecchi
(The Increase of His Government)

> "To really walk in truth we need the scriptures and the power of God. Not one or the other, but both."
>
> Adam LiVecchi
> (Listen.Learn.Obey)

"The moment you were born again you became like Jesus: a gift for the world to receive."

Aaron LiVecchi

> "Often our silence keeps others trapped in darkness."
>
> Adam LiVecchi
> (Rediscovering the Prophetic)

"Captivity always follows disobedience."

Adam LiVecchi
(Sitting at His Feet)

"Change is very uncomfortable to most people because we have to give up control."

Adam LiVecchi
(So You Want To Change The World)

"God's truth sets us free, and His kindness keeps us free."

Aaron LiVecchi

> "The Kingdom of God is the only government with an incorruptible justice system."
>
> Sarah LiVecchi

> "We need to see the world through the eyes of Jesus."
>
> Adam LiVecchi
> (The Increase of His Government)

> "Radical obedience is the simplest definition of a Kingdom lifestyle."
>
> Adam LiVecchi
> (The Increase of His Government)

"The deeper the sanctification we go through, the purer we reflect Jesus to those around us."

Adam LiVecchi
(His Name is the Word of God)

"Trust is a wineskin for understanding."

Adam LiVecchi
(Follow.Lead.Mentor)

"Wisdom is the facilitator of purpose, destiny, and success."

Adam LiVecchi
(The Increase of His Government)

> "To walk by faith and walk in love implies that we go somewhere."
>
> Aaron LiVecchi

> "Mercy is not getting what we deserve; grace is getting what we don't deserve."
>
> Adam LiVecchi
> (His Name is the Word of God)

> "Grace is released in the time of need, and it helps to accomplish something both in us and through us."
>
> Adam LiVecchi
> (The Increase of His Government)

> "Sympathy wishes for the best. Love becomes a solution."
>
> Aaron LiVecchi

> "When the veil of Jesus' flesh was torn, we were all invited to live in the Secret Place forever."
>
> Adam LiVecchi
> (So You Want To Change The World)

"Don't let your condition define your identity."

Sarah LiVecchi

> "There are things that people are waiting on God for and He's actually waiting on us."
>
> Adam LiVecchi
> (The Increase of His Government)

> "If you want to be a person who is trustworthy and has integrity, accountability is a must."
>
> Adam LiVecchi
> (Follow.Lead.Mentor)

> "We have been given the mind of Christ therefore we can have a continual eternal perspective."
>
> Adam LiVecchi
> (Rediscovering the Prophetic)

"As long as you keep your eyes on Jesus you will be able to walk on water."

Jamie Centeno

"Hope sees opportunities."

Adam LiVecchi

"Your personal history with God will determine your future."

Abner Suarez

"Properly handling inconvenience cultivates character."

Aaron LiVecchi

" You are Salt - for Preservation.
You are Light - for Revelation.
You are Leaven - for Infiltration."

Adam LiVecchi

> "When Jesus speaks to us, He's actually forming Himself in us."
>
> Adam LiVecchi
> (His Name is the Word of God)

> "To live we must hear because faith comes by hearing, and the just live by faith."
>
> Adam LiVecchi
> (Sitting at His Feet)

> "Language identifies your location."
>
> David Greco

"The key that opens every door is intimacy with Jesus."

Adam LiVecchi
(Go.Preach.Heal)

> "His word has to find residence in us if Jesus is going to be preeminent in our lives."
>
> Adam LiVecchi
> (His Name is the Word of God)

"The last wall in the woman's heart at the well's heart was religion."

Nic Billman

> "A life of faith is consistently reaching beyond where you are with what you are reaching for in view."
>
> Adam LiVecchi

"In our walk with God there are things God changes and things we are to change. God will not do our job and we cannot do his."

Adam LiVecchi
(Rediscovering the Prophetic)

> "Wisdom gives you a message. Integrity makes you a message."
>
> Aaron LiVecchi

"One of the keys to success at almost anything is you must give what you are doing your undivided attention while you are doing it."

Adam LiVecchi
(Follow.Lead.Mentor)

> "A Kingdom worldview is necessary if we are going to live in the world and not be of the world."
>
> Adam LiVecchi
> (The Increase of His Government)

> "God doesn't give you more than you can handle. The most difficult situation is God showing His confidence in what He put in you."
>
> Aaron LiVecchi

"When we learn to abide in Christ beyond our emotions then Jesus will overflow from our lives onto the world around us."

Adam LiVecchi
(Go.Preach.Heal)

"The sacrifice of learning leads to the responsibility of teaching and the privilege of being a teacher."

Adam LiVecchi
(Listen.Learn.Obey)

> "Religion demands, God gives."
>
> David Greco

> "Spiritual hunger will cause you to put your life in order."
>
> Adam LiVecchi

> "Religion always tries to complicate what God has made plain, or explain what God has kept hidden."
>
> Adam LiVecchi
> (Rediscovering the Prophetic)

> "God is naturally supernatural. When we hear and obey God, we become naturally supernatural."
>
> Adam LiVecchi
> (Sitting at His Feet)

> "As the Word is dividing our soul and spirit, it is then that discernment grows and deepens in us."
>
> Adam LiVecchi
> (His Name is the Word of God)

"Leaders should always be the initiators of reconciliation."

Adam LiVecchi
(Follow.Lead.Mentor)

> "Faithfulness and perseverance will cause promotion in the Kingdom."
>
> Adam LiVecchi
> (Sitting at His Feet)

"It is only in obeying his commands that we abide in him. You cannot abide in him and disobey his commands; it is just not possible."

Adam LiVecchi
(Go.Preach.Heal)

> "We don't earn anything in the Kingdom of God."
>
> Abner Suarez

"Faith is to expect the impossible."

Adam LiVecchi

> "God is really smart he does everything for a reason. Nothing is spontaneous to God he is intentional about everything he says and does."
>
> Adam LiVecchi
> (Rediscovering the Prophetic)

> "Obeying what we do not understand is God's way of preparing us for a blessing we cannot contain."
>
> Adam LiVecchi
> (Sitting at His Feet)

"Hell on earth is not hearing God's voice."

Adam LiVecchi
(Sitting at His Feet)

> "The cross is not only to be carried, but studied, and experienced."
>
> Adam LiVecchi
> (The Execution of Jesus Christ)

> "People who have experience with Jesus love to speak about it, people that lack experience like to debate and accuse others."
>
> Adam LiVecchi
> (His Name is the Word of God)

"As Jesus commands us to do something, His authority can flow through our submission."

Adam LiVecchi
(The Increase of His Government)

> "The key to living a life that is naturally productive, spiritually fruitful and just plain interesting is learning."
>
> Adam LiVecchi
> (Listen.Learn.Obey)

"God gives us what we don't deserve expecting us to go and do likewise."

Aaron LiVecchi

> "False assumptions can lead to unnecessary disappointment."
>
> Adam LiVecchi
> (Follow.Lead.Mentor)

> "The world around us receives revelation of Christ Jesus through our words, actions and lifestyles."
>
> Adam LiVecchi
> (Rediscovering the Prophetic)

"When we obey God's word, we put on the Lord Jesus Christ."

Adam LiVecchi
(Sitting at His Feet)

"All authentic ministry proceeds from the secret place."

Adam LiVecchi
(Listen.Learn.Obey)

> "When we learn to die to self is when we learn how to love God and our neighbor."
>
> Adam LiVecchi
> (The Execution of Jesus Christ)

"People must matter more to us than what they can do for us."

Adam LiVecchi

> "Our first love will always be our first focus, what we are focused on, we are filled with."
>
> Adam LiVecchi
> (His Name is the Word of God)

> "God will often reach out to a society to the same extent we are willing to."
>
> Aaron LiVecchi

> "Ministry happens every time we say yes to Jesus and obey him."
>
> Adam LiVecchi
> (Go.Preach.Heal)

> "Hearing directly deals with the affections. The more we love someone the more we will listen to him or her."
>
> Adam LiVecchi
> (Sitting at His Feet)

> "Sickness is to your body as sin is to your soul, Jesus bled for both."
>
> Adam LiVecchi

"The most valuable things in life are not for sale."

Adam LiVecchi

> "People who want to walk in deep revelation must be willing to stand with others."
>
> Adam LiVecchi
> (Rediscovering the Prophetic)

"When the Word is flesh in us, it is then when our Christianity becomes visible to those around us."

Adam LiVecchi
(His Name is the Word of God)

> "While we procrastinate, the enemy assassinates."
>
> Adam LiVecchi
> (Follow.Lead.Mentor)

> "We need to stop talking departure and start talking dominion."
>
> Bishop Michael Pitts

"If the gates of hell are prevailing its not the church."

Adam LiVecchi

"Our intimacy with Jesus is seen in our love for people."

Adam LiVecchi
(Rediscovering the Prophetic)

"Contentment is wrapped up in the truth that Jesus will never leave us nor forsake us."

Adam LiVecchi
(His Name is the Word of God)

"Listening precedes leading."

Adam LiVecchi
(Follow.Lead.Mentor)

> "Listening is wanting to hear."
>
> (Anonymous High School Student)

> "When the gospel is received, spiritual sight is received."
>
> Adam LiVecchi
> (The Increase of His Government)

"Many times people want to lead but have never really learned to follow."

Adam LiVecchi
(Follow.Lead.Mentor)

> "The Kingdom of God is at hand."
>
> Jesus Christ

> "The way we get promoted in our destiny is by serving someone else in his or hers."
>
> Adam LiVecchi
> (Sitting at His Feet)

"Abiding in him and him abiding in us is a work of the Holy Spirit but also a participation of our will and choices."

Adam LiVecchi
(Go.Preach.Heal)

> "God's Jealousy for us is what empowers us to pursue him."
>
> Adam LiVecchi

"The posture of a learner is one of humility."

Adam LiVecchi
(Listen.Learn.Obey)

> "The mysteries of the Kingdom are about the King, for everything in the Kingdom is a reflection of the King."
>
> Adam LiVecchi
> (The Execution of Jesus Christ)

"Jesus delights to delegate authority to us so that we can live in submission to His mission."

Adam LiVecchi
(The Increase of His Government)

> "A rebuke that doesn't involve an invitation to grow is just criticism."
>
> Aaron LiVecchi

> "A prepared heart will often be expressed in a courageous life of one who isn't afraid to go against the flow."
>
> Adam LiVecchi
> (Rediscovering the Prophetic)

> "Your sense of need for God is actually your fountain of revelation from God."
>
> Adam LiVecchi

> "Abundant life is not measured in dollars and cents but in us hearing God and obeying Him."
>
> Adam LiVecchi
> (Sitting at His Feet)

> "To really walk in truth our theology must become part of our life story."
>
> Adam LiVecchi
> (Go.Preach.Heal)

> "We don't interpret the Bible; the Bible interprets the Bible."
>
> Adam LiVecchi
> (Listen.Learn.Obey)

> "Perseverance is patience in motion."
>
> Adam LiVecchi
> (The Increase of His Government)

"Faith comes by hearing, but unbelief grows by not listening."

Adam LiVecchi
(Rediscovering the Prophetic)

"You can't build on image it's hollow, but you can build on substance."

Adam LiVecchi

"Real and long-lasting change starts on the inside."

Adam LiVecchi
(So You Want To Change The World)

> "God is faithful, by whom ye were called unto the fellowship of his Son Jesus Christ our Lord."
>
> I Corinthians 1:9

> "We are only as filled as much as we overflow onto others."
>
> Adam LiVecchi
> (His Name is the Word of God)

"In the Kingdom we don't build walls we build bridges."

Adam LiVecchi
(Go.Preach.Heal)

"A listening ear will turn a coward courageous."

Adam LiVecchi
(Rediscovering the Prophetic)

> "Those who are really filled naturally overflow."
>
> Adam LiVecchi
> (Rediscovering the Prophetic)

"Salvation is not just having a Savior, but it is also having a Lord."

Adam LiVecchi
(Go.Preach.Heal)

> "Unbelief is to question God's integrity."
>
> Steve Stewart

> "When we live with a biblical understanding of urgency, it causes us to live faithfully with what God has entrusted us with today."
>
> Adam LiVecchi
> (The Increase of His Government)

"There is no compromise in the wisdom that comes from the mouth of the Lord Jesus Christ."

Adam LiVecchi
(The Increase of His Government)

"A tender heart is one that is not offended"

Adam LiVecchi
(His Name is the Word of God)

> "Christianity is having a revelation of Jesus Christ and giving it away."
>
> Adam LiVecchi
> (So You Want To Change The World)

"The revelation of the Lamb will come to those who have surrendered hearts and want more of God."

Adam LiVecchi
(His Name is the Word of God)

> "The simplicity of Christ is the wineskin in which God can pour the mysteries of Christ in."
>
> Adam LiVecchi
> (The Execution of Jesus Christ)

"Moral absolutes give your soul boundaries."

Adam LiVecchi

> "To faithfully steward what God desires to entrust to us, self-control is a must."
>
> Adam LiVecchi
> (Follow.Lead.Mentor)

"God uses His authority to release creativity in the midst of our assignment."

Adam LiVecchi
(The Increase of His Government)

> "If we are not willing to give up control, we are not willing to follow Jesus."
>
> Adam LiVecchi
> (So You Want To Change The World)

"We can change the world around us because He has changed the world in us."

Adam LiVecchi
(So You Want To Change The World)

> "The Church doesn't have a mission, the mission has a church."
>
> Steve Stewart

"Religion always tries to box people in but God is in the business of sending people out."

Adam LiVecchi
(Rediscovering the Prophetic)

"When Jesus told us to go into all the world and preach the gospel, it was a commandment not a suggestion"

Adam LiVecchi
(Go.Preach.Heal)

"God doesn't just want His people out of Egypt; He wants Egypt out of His people."

Adam LiVecchi
(His Name is the Word of God)

> "Often Heaven breaks in when all hell breaks loose."
>
> Aaron LiVecchi

> "Understanding the necessity of hearing God's voice will give birth to wisdom; wisdom is received as we hear God speak."
>
> Adam LiVecchi
> (Sitting at His Feet)

> "Leadership is about consistently doing what you already know to do."
>
> Adam LiVecchi

> "The mysteries of the Kingdom are not hidden from us but are hidden for us."
>
> Bill Johnson

> "Real ministry is when people see Jesus through our obedience to His word."
>
> Adam LiVecchi
> (So You Want To Change The World)

> "Humility and honor create a great atmosphere for learning."
>
> Adam LiVecchi
> (Listen.Learn.Obey)

> "God's sovereignty delegates authority to us so we can fulfill His desires."
>
> Adam LiVecchi
> (The Increase of His Government)

"There are conditions if we want to follow Jesus.
We cannot serve God on our own terms"

Adam LiVecchi
(The Execution of Jesus Christ)

"Often the preparation determines the outcome."

Adam LiVecchi
(Rediscovering the Prophetic)

"Wise virgins are those who sit at the feet of Jesus and cultivate a hearing ear and a burning heart."

Adam LiVecchi
(His Name is the Word of God)

> "There is no real Christianity without the Secret Place."
>
> Adam LiVecchi
> (So You Want To Change The World)

"Every time God reveals something to you it is him saying, "Papa loves you and doesn't want you to be in the dark."

Adam LiVecchi
(Rediscovering the Prophetic)

> "You can not make decisions based on knowledge you do not have."
>
> Pastor Scott Pursley

> "Jesus overcame the temptation of identity-based performance; therefore we must live in His victory which was for us."
>
> Adam LiVecchi
> (The Execution of Jesus Christ)

> "A hearing ear and a burning heart will lead to a lifestyle of obedience to God's word and outpourings of His Spirit."
>
> Adam LiVecchi
> (His Name is the Word of God)

> "Mercy picks us up when we fall while grace gives us strength to stand."
>
> Adam LiVecchi

> "We manage the freedom we have been given by making healthy choices."
>
> Aaron LiVecchi

"When you have a biblical worldview, false doctrine can be discerned."

Adam LiVecchi
(The Increase of His Government)

> "The atmosphere of our life should be defined by the voice of the Lord."
>
> Adam LiVecchi
> (Rediscovering the Prophetic)

"Often people lack spiritual authority because their life style and the actions are not in agreement."

Adam LiVecchi
(Listen.Learn.Obey)

"When we are His reflection, those who are not looking for Him find Him in us, that is Christianity."

Adam LiVecchi
(His Name is the Word of God)

"Integrity gives us the right to influence others."

Adam LiVecchi

> "The art of hearing is developed when we learn the discipline of listening."
>
> Adam LiVecchi
> (Sitting at His feet)

"Do all the good you can, by all the means you can, in all the ways you can, in all the places you can, at all the times you can, to all the people you can, as long as ever you can."

John Wesley

> "Relationships in the Kingdom of God are more than a lifetime; they are eternal."
>
> Adam LiVecchi
> (The Increase of His Government)

"We serve and He brings us into places of influence."

Adam LiVecchi
(His Name is the Word of God)

> "Out of the abundance of the heart, the mouth speaks. To be intentional with your words, you have to start being intentional with your heart."
>
> Aaron LiVecchi

> "Destiny begins when we are willing to lose control and comfort and follow the Lord."
>
> Adam LiVecchi
> (Rediscovering the Prophetic)

> "When we approach God with reverence, we are positioning ourselves for revelation."
>
> Adam LiVecchi
> (Sitting at His Feet)

"Jesus is only our Lord if we hear His word and obey it."

Adam LiVecchi
(His Name is the Word of God)

> "To walk in the truth we need a listening ear."
>
> Adam LiVecchi
> (Rediscovering the Prophetic)

> "The Father is throwing a wedding party for His Son and you are invited, that is the best news you will ever hear."
>
> Adam LiVecchi
> (Rediscovering the Prophetic)

"When someone has expectation, they take risks."

Aaron LiVecchi

"Thou hast put all things in subjection under his feet. For in that he put all in subjection under him, he left nothing that is not put under him. But now we see not yet all things put under him."
Hebrews 2:8

> "But we see Jesus, who was made a little lower than the angels for the suffering of death, crowned with glory and honour; that he by the grace of God should taste death for every man."
> Hebrews 2:9

Newest Book by Adam LiVecchi

More Titles from Adam LiVecchi
His Name is the Word of God *(also in Spanish)*
So You Want to Change the World *(with Destiny Image)*
The Execution of Jesus Christ
Go.Preach.Heal *(also in Spanish, Portuguese, and Russian)*
Listen.Learn.Obey *(with John Natale)*
Sitting at His Feet
The Increase of His Government
Rediscovering the Prophetic

Available at www.WeSeeJesusMinistries.com

www.ingramcontent.com/pod-product-compliance
Lightning Source LLC
Chambersburg PA
CBHW030442300426
44112CB00009B/1124